The EVERYTHING KIDS' MORE Hidden Pictures BOOK

Discover hours of fun with over 100 brand-new puzzles!

Beth L. Blair

Aadamsmedia

Avon, Massachusetts

Dedication

To Jenny, who inspires me to work hard and be on time.
While I don't always succeed, you always make me try. With love and thanks, Beth

PUBLISHER Karen Cooper

DIRECTOR OF ACQUISITIONS AND INNOVATION Paula Munier

MANAGING EDITOR, EVERYTHING® SERIES Lisa Laing

COPY CHIEF Casey Ebert

ACQUISITIONS EDITOR Katrina Schroeder

SENIOR DEVELOPMENT EDITOR Brett Palana-Shanahan

ASSOCIATE DEVELOPMENT EDITOR Hillary Thompson

EDITORIAL ASSISTANT Ross Weisman

EVERYTHING® SERIES COVER DESIGNER Erin Alexander

LAYOUT DESIGNERS Colleen Cunningham, Elisabeth Lariviere, Ashley Vierra, Denise Wallace

An Everything® Series Book.
Everything® and everything.com® are registered trademarks of F+W Media, Inc.

Published by Adams Media, an F+W Media Company
57 Littlefield Street, Avon, MA 02322. U.S.A.
www.adamsmedia.com

ISBN 10: 1-4405-0614-0
ISBN 13: 978-1-4405-0614-7
eISBN 10: 1-4405-0615-9
eISBN 13: 978-1-4405-0615-4

Printed by RR Donnelley, Harrisonburg, VA, USA.
August 2010

10 9 8 7 6 5 4 3 2 1

This publication is designed to provide accurate and authoritative information with regard to the subject matter covered. It is sold with the understanding that the publisher is not engaged in rendering legal, accounting, or other professional advice. If legal advice or other expert assistance is required, the services of a competent professional person should be sought.
—From a *Declaration of Principles* jointly adopted by a Committee of the American Bar Association and a Committee of Publishers and Associations

Many of the designations used by manufacturers and sellers to distinguish their products are claimed as trademarks. When those designations appear in this book and Adams Media was aware of a trademark claim, the designations have been printed with initial capital letters.

Interior illustrations by Kurt Dolber.
Puzzles by Beth L. Blair.

This book is available at quantity discounts for bulk purchases.
For information, please call 1-800-289-0963.

Visit the entire Everything® series at *www.everything.com*

CONTENTS

INTRODUCTION

Welcome to The Everything® Kids' More Hidden Pictures Book!

As an artist, creating hidden picture puzzles is one of my favorite things to do. Why? Because I get to be sneaky. You may think you are looking at a picture of just one thing, but really there are a whole bunch of smaller pictures just waiting to be discovered. A boy's curly hair is actually a curly sheep, a patch on a pair of jeans is really a high-flying kite with a long tail, and bananas and teacups are lurking everywhere!

It takes some thinking, a lot of erasing, and a bit of redrawing to turn a nose into a trumpet or a bunch of tree branches into a king's crown. It is even harder to hide an entire elephant in the pattern of a beautiful dress! But if you study any picture long enough, the shapes start to look like other things. Suddenly a coat sleeve looks like a wrinkled sock, and a flower looks like a butterfly. After a while, it becomes easy to sneak extra pictures in everywhere.

I hope you enjoy finding all the crazy things that I've hidden for you in *The Everything® Kids' More Hidden Pictures Book*. Just remember—you can never be 100% sure what you are seeing because I am really, really sneaky!

Happy hunting,

Beth L. Blair

Beth L. Blair

P.S. Check the following page for a puzzle to get you started. You might want to grab a supply of brightly colored markers. They will make it easy for you to highlight the hidden pictures once you have found them.

I chose these horses
because they are both
covered with big spots.
It is easy to hide things
in this kind of pattern!

Ready? There are
16 items that you
need to find.

ARROW HAMMER MITTEN BOWLING PIN

SOCK KITE BALLOON SMOKING PIPE

HEART CAR FLOWER PINE TREE

TEACUP FISH LETTER H QUESTION MARK

CHAPTER 1

Playtime

Go Fish

Can you tell who is winning this round of Go Fish? While you figure that out, see if you can find the 9 fish hiding in this picture.

Sneak Attack!

These two brothers play the same game every night—who can sneak close enough to Dad to tickle him with the feather? While they sneak, take a peek and see if you can find these 9 items hiding in the room: **baseball**, **comb**, **envelope**, **golf club**, **matchstick**, **birdhouse**, **kite**, **capital letter F**, and **snail**.

Hot pepper, hot pepper, 1, 2, 3, find these items quick as can be: **flag**, **bird**, **fish**, **pizza slice**, **vase of flowers**, **balloon**, and **needle**.

Jump Rope

Ooey Gooey

Janey and Bev just love to play in the mud! Can you find the 8 items hiding in their mushy masterpiece? Look for a **pocket watch**, **spatula**, **spoon**, **sock**, **comb**, **mug**, **birthday candle**, **needle and thread**.

Round and Round

When the music stops, these three kids will scramble to see who gets the two chairs! Can you find 12 items hiding in this picture before one of these kids is O-U-T out? Look for a **fish hook**, **ruler**, **slice of pizza**, **ice cream cone**, **umbrella**, **mushroom**, **sock**, **daisy**, **big musical note**, **heart**, **postage stamp**, and **teacup**.

Driveway Art

Tony has an under-the-sea theme going down the driveway.
He's drawing a whale right now, but can you also find
the **fish**, **eel**, **crab**, **starfish**, **scallop shell**, **seahorse**,
and **jellyfish** that are hidden on this page?

Choo Choo

Emma and Ryan like to take out the trains and cars and spread out all over the living room floor! Can you find these 10 items hiding on the facing page with all the toys? You are looking for a **chicken**, **teacup**, **2 cat faces**, **leaf**, **comb**, **letter X**, **smiley face**, **paper clip**, and **slice of pizza**.

Goal!

Soccer can be a mad scramble to run after the ball and try to score a point. How many times can you find the complete word **G-O-A-L** hiding among the flying feet?

The Champ

Gramps is the best tiddlywinker in the family! While he is using the squidger (*big disk*) to shoot the winks (*small disks*), see if you can find a **jump rope**, **candle**, **Christmas tree**, **needle and thread**, **leaf**, **pencil**, **smiley face**, **pear**, **flag**, **caterpillar**, and **music note**.

ZAP!

These two brothers are trying to see who can get the most points playing this computer game. You can play, too! See how many times you can find the word Z-A-P hiding in the border of this page. Multiply the number of ZAPs by 10 to get your score. The brothers' top score so far is 90. Did you beat them?

Flashlight Tag

Rebecca is trying to sneak past Andrew and make it "home" before he can tag her with a beam of light. See if you can find the 13 items hiding in the dark with the other kids! Look for a **pair of dice**, **comb**, **book**, **capital M**, **umbrella**, **candle**, **balloon**, **kite**, **glove**, **pencil**, **snake**, **eyeglasses**, and **a sock**.

CHAPTER 2

Hobbies

Swim Team

Being on your neighborhood or school swim team is a great hobby! But look out before you dive in this pool—there are 9 things here that don't belong in the water or pool area. Can you find them? Look for a **snake**, **piece of bacon**, **flag**, **spoon**, **tulip**, **needle and thread**, **shoe with laces**, **hot dog with mustard**, and a **candy cane**.

Zip Zip

Slot cars are tiny little racers that can zip around a plastic track at super fast speeds. Lots of kids, and adults, too, like to collect and race them! See if you can find a **lemon slice, playing card, pencil, glasses, toothbrush, nail, slice of Swiss cheese,** and a **ruler.**

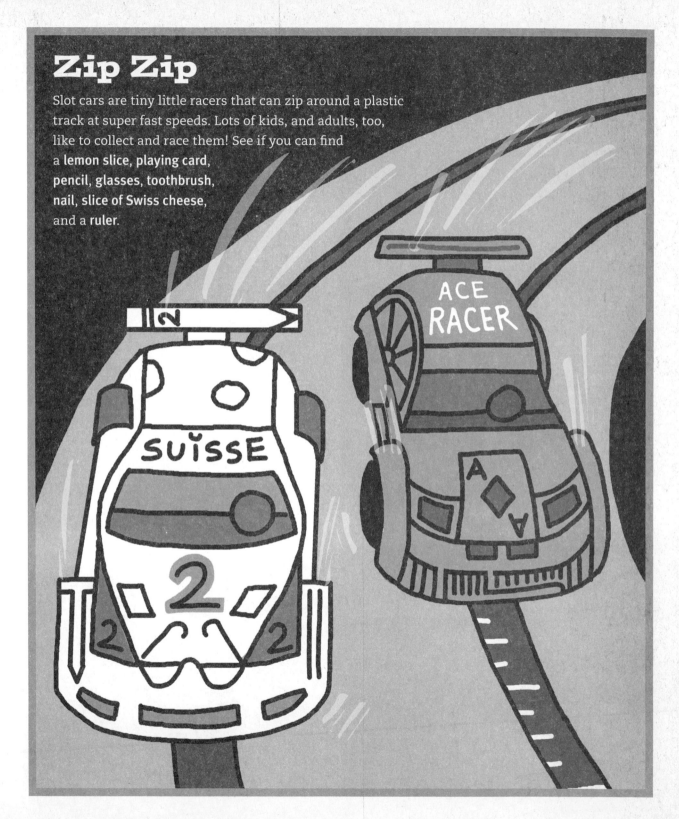

Love to Bake

Carmen and John bake whenever they can. Today they are making sugar cookies, but who knows what they might bake tomorrow? Help them find the extra ingredients, baked goods, and kitchen tools hiding in this picture. You are looking for a **fork**, **pretzel**, **tablespoon**, **teacup**, **muffin**, **stick of butter**, **strawberry**, and a **slice of pie**.

Pet Me, Please

Willow has a lot of animal friends to take care of. You can see 5 of them here, all waiting their turn for some attention. Can you find 5 more hiding in the picture? Look for a **parrot**, **fancy goldfish**, **turtle**, **snake**, and **bunny**.

Fuzzy Friends

Sammi loves fuzzy things! She collects fuzzy stuffed animals, wears fuzzy clothes, and even has a fuzzy pet! See if you can find the following fuzzy things hiding on the fuzzy facing page:

—a pair of fuzzy socks
—a pair of fuzzy mittens
—a fuzzy chick
—13 tiny fuzzy teddy bears

EXTRA FUN: Can you find Sammi, too?

Feed the Birds

Keisha makes sure the birds in her yard have plenty of seed and water. If she's very quiet, birds will come to the feeder while she is standing there! See if you can find what else is at the feeder today. Look for a **lady's profile**, **bunny**, **pair of dice**, **heart**, **mitten**, **crown**, and, of course, a **bird**.

Tumble Bug

Marta practices her tumbling as often as she can. Usually the gym is crowded, but today it looks pretty empty. Wait a minute—there are 10 items hiding in the gym with Marta! Can you find a **bowling pin**, **kite**, **sheet of notebook paper**, **mitten**, **balloon**, **candy cane**, **needle and thread**, **pencil**, **clock**, and **umbrella**? After you find them all, do a somersault to celebrate!

Making Music

This girl loves to play her F-I-D-D-L-E. Find the letters for her instrument hiding in this picture along with a **banana peel**, **paintbrush**, **winter hat**, **flag**, and a **fork**.

Busy With Blocks

Brian can get lost for hours building cities and castles. If he runs out of blocks, he uses whatever is handy! He needed lots of extra parts to finish this cityscape. See if you can find an **umbrella**, **capital letters N and L**, **playing card**, **lemon slice**, **birdhouse**, **comb**, **single dice**, **pizza slice**, **Christmas tree**, **book**, **man's face**, **camera**, and a **ruler**.

Crazy for Quilting

People who love to quilt have been "bitten by the quilting bug." These girls designed their own quilting bug—a butterfly! How many butterfly blocks can you find in this quilt top? Hint: There are two different butterfly patterns.

Model Kid

Jacob likes to put together and paint all kinds of
models. What is he working on today? Follow the
color key to fill in the outlines and see!

B - BLACK   G - GREEN
R - RED   Y - YELLOW
S - SKIN

CHAPTER 3

What Will I Be?

I Like to Help Animals

When you grow up, maybe you will be a veterinarian
or a zookeeper! While you think about that,
see if you can find the **light bulb**, **fish**,
bowling pin, **snake**, **heart**, **fried egg**,
quarter, and **oven mitt**.

Look for:

CLOCK WHISTLE
TRUMPET

BOOT HEART
MATCHES CAMPFIRE
PINE TREE SMILE FACE
RUBBER DUCK STAR
COMB
ARROW

I Like to Race

Someone who has a need for speed could be a race car driver, extreme athlete, or even an astronaut!

I Like to Act

Some performers start out very young! While you wait for your big break, find a **candle**, **two butterflies**, **slice of cake**, **paperclip**, **needle and thread**, **golf club**, **feather**, **Christmas stocking**, **playing card**, and **teacup**.

I Like to Fish

Sam (short for Samantha) loves to be out on the water with her dad. Maybe she will be a conservationist or park ranger! Look for the 9 outdoor items: **spider**, **bunny**, **kite**, **mushroom**, **leaf**, **pine tree**, **river**, **cloud**, and **shell**.

GO FISH

1st

I Like to Draw

Creative people can have many different careers. They could be cartoonists, animators, painters, art teachers, or fabric designers—and that's just a few of their choices! See if you can find the 9 items that this girl had to draw in her art class.

Look for:
BIRD
APPLE
PEAR
BANANA
TWO FACES
LANDSCAPE
TEAPOT
LIGHTBULB

I Like to Teach

If you like to teach, you might someday work in an elementary or high school. You might even be a college professor! Meanwhile, can you help this big brother show the alphabet to his little sister?

I Like to Fly

Brendan dreams of becoming an airline pilot one day. While he's thinking about the future, see if you can help him find 13 things that go UP: a **rocket**, **hot air balloon**, **bird**, **star**, **helium balloon**, **kite**, **paper airplane**, **arrow**, **flag**, and **4 bubbles**.

I Like to Play With Hair

Can you find the 1 pair of scissors that these poor dolls have hidden from this future hairdresser?

I Like to See How Things Work

Jesse is always taking apart old machines and electronics. He likes to discover how the different wires, knobs, and gears connect to make things work. When Jesse grows up, he would make a great engineer or mechanic.

Look for:

HAMMER

SCREWDRIVER

WRENCH

LIGHT BULB

PLIERS

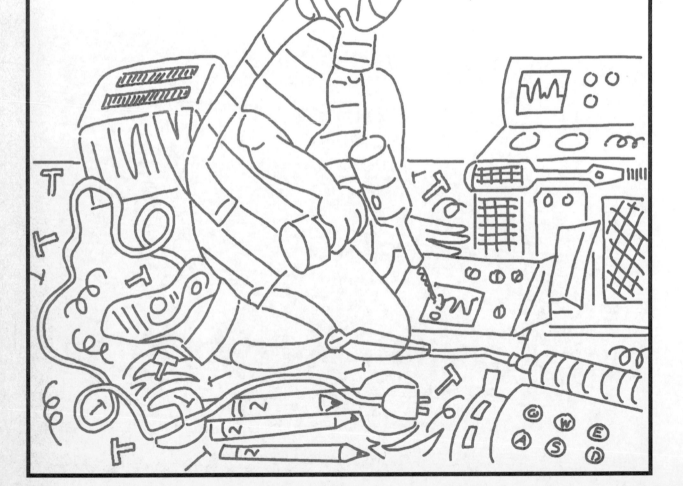

I Like to Save the World

You could grow up to be a real superhero by becoming a firefighter, policeman, or EMT! Look for **2 super bats**, **2 super spiders**, **2 super Ws**, and **5 super stars**.

I Like to Sell Things

Think of all the things that people buy, from ice cream to automobiles. Someone has to sell them! Help this future salesperson find a **teacup**, **teapot**, **chicken leg**, **banana**, **playing card**, **comb**, **boot**, **pencil**, **paperclip**, **hamster**, **T-shirt**, and a **pineapple**.

CHAPTER 4

Fantasy

Wicked Witches

These witches are brewing up a pot of invisibility potion. Can you find the 13 items they've hidden all over this page? Look for a **burning candle**, **skull**, **banana**, **frog**, **ice skate**, **wineglass**, two **bats**, **cat**, **house**, **strip of bacon**, **light bulb**, and a **spider**.

Santa's Elves

Santa's workshop is bustling all year round with busy elves working hard to get ready for Christmas! In addition to all the toys, see if you can find a **coat hanger**, **ice cream cone**, **kite**, **toothbrush**, **clock**, **teapot**, **toucan**, **capital letter E**, **playing card**, and **Santa** himself!

Jack and the Giant

Look for an **ice cream cone**, **heart**, **teacup**, **pair of eyeglasses**, **trident**, **paper clip**, **shamrock**, **balloon**, and a **crown**.

Groaning Ghosts

How many ghosts can you find hiding
in this haunted picture?

EXTRA FUN:
Where is the
pair of ghostly
gloves?

R.I.P.

Under the Sea

See if you can guess what kind of book the mermaid is reading to her friends. The list of objects hidden in this picture will give you a hint! Look for a **slice of bread**, **egg**, **bowl of pasta**, **muffin**, **lemon slice**, **banana**, **spoonful of oatmeal**, and a **bottle of oil**.

Uniquely Unicorn

This fantastic creature is one of a kind! Not only did he step out of the pages of a storybook, he brought along 12 hidden items. Look for a **comb**, **wishbone**, **snake**, **teacup**, **swim flipper**, **butterfly**, **glove**, **magnet**, **telephone receiver**, **heart**, **pair of scissors**, and a **paintbrush**.

Fairy Godmother

This tiny fairy godmother helped the princess get dressed for a party. She also used her magic to hide 11 items in this picture! Look for a **pair of swim flippers, capital letter Y, teapot, whale, house painting brush, umbrella, banana, penguin, fried egg,** and a **pumpkin.**

Lucky Leprechauns

It's easy to mistake one leprechaun for another since they look so much alike. However, there are 6 silly differences between these two. Can you spot them?

EXTRA FUN:
Leprechauns are very good at making shoes. Can you find the pair of buckle shoes hiding in this picture? The shoes the leprechauns are wearing don't count.

Dragon's Den

Dragons like to heap their stolen treasures into a big messy pile. What kind of crazy treasures can you find in this dragon's den? There's no list of items, but there are over 40 things to find!

3 Wishes

This genie grants wishes in multiples of three.
See if you can find either 3 or 6 of these items: **snakes**,
coat hangers, **fish**, **bananas**, and the **number 3**!

Terrible Troll

This troll thinks he is hiding where the sun can't reach him. Can you find the 8 sunshines that have followed him underground?

EXTRA FUN: Not only sunshine makes a troll run and hide. See if you can find a toothbrush, toothpaste, bar of soap, and a comb!

CHAPTER 5

Time Travel

Let's Go!

Wouldn't it be fun to have a magic hat that would let you travel through time? Let's follow Ethan on a few of his adventures. Before we go, find 11 devices that measure time. Look carefully—some are new and a few are VERY old!

Dinosaur Days

Ethan isn't sure he has the best snack for a raptor! Can you find another food this dinosaur might like? Look for a **hotdog in a bun**, **hamburger**, **slice of pepperoni pizza**, **elbow macaroni**, **fried egg**, **strip of bacon**, **gingerbread man**, **slice of pie**, **ice cream cone**, **chicken leg**, **muffin**, and a **banana**.

Ancient Egypt

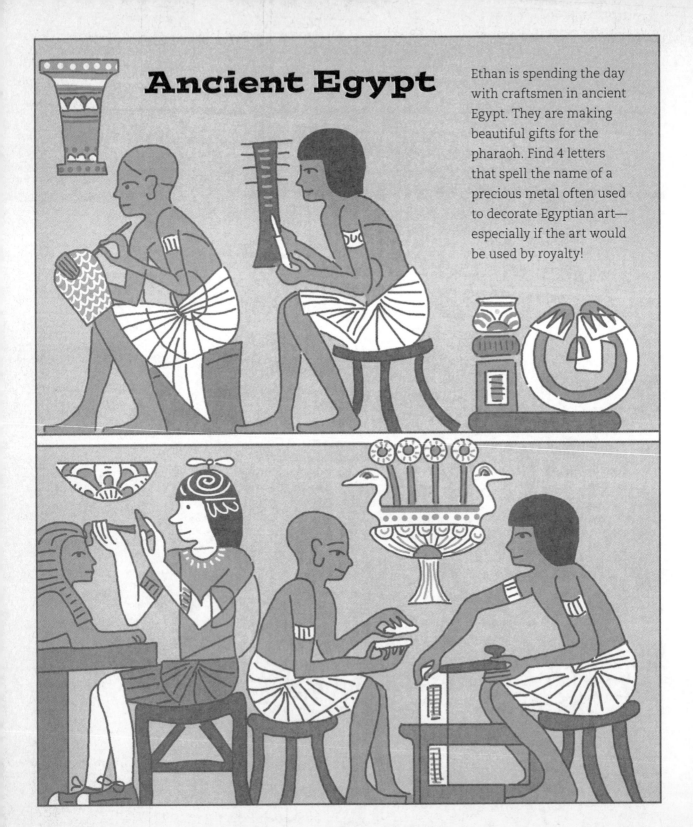

Ethan is spending the day with craftsmen in ancient Egypt. They are making beautiful gifts for the pharaoh. Find 4 letters that spell the name of a precious metal often used to decorate Egyptian art—especially if the art would be used by royalty!

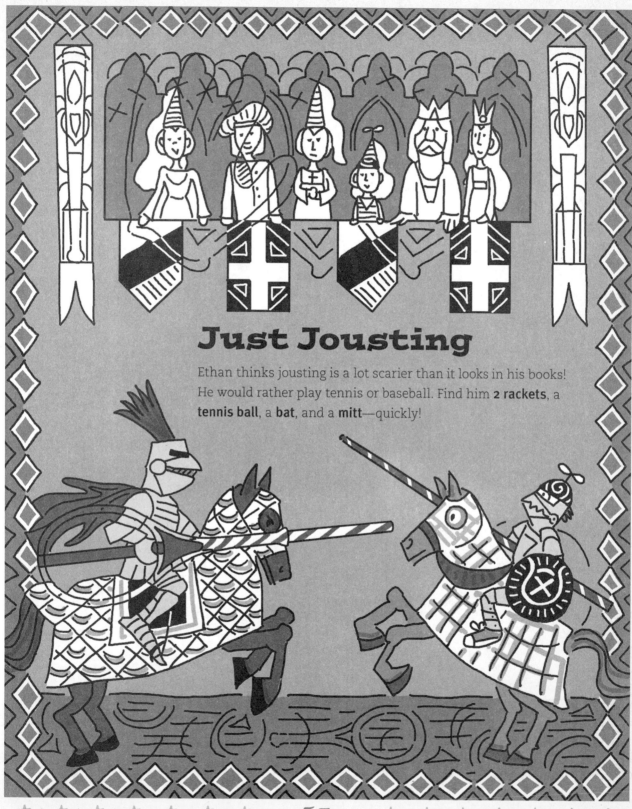

Just Jousting

Ethan thinks jousting is a lot scarier than it looks in his books! He would rather play tennis or baseball. Find him **2 rackets**, a **tennis ball**, a **bat**, and a **mitt**—quickly!

Antique Car

Ethan got a driving lesson when he traveled back to 1905. This car was new at the time, but it seems to be missing the roof and windshield! The shape is also very different from a modern car. Can you find 6 sleek cars from today hiding in this scene?

Great Galileo

It was just over 400 years ago that an astronomer named Galileo built a telescope and proved that the planets in our solar system, including Earth, circle around the sun. Ethan wanted just one peek through Galileo's famous telescope. Guess what? The moon looked just the same as it does today! Can you find the **13 crescent moons** and **3 five-pointed stars** in this night scene?

Mr. President

President Abraham Lincoln thinks he is reading with his son Tad, but look again! Can you find 10 books for Abe and Ethan?

Oh, Blots!

Ethan thought that going to school in the 1800s would be easy. Today the class is learning how to write with a quill, and he thinks it's hard! Can you find 7 pencils for the kids to use?

Is Anybody Home?

This beautiful forest is in a time long before people.
Find 15 things that people will invent some day.
There are things for work, travel, and fun.
There are some favorite foods, too!

Magic Time

Throughout history, some people have claimed to have special powers. Do they really, or are magicians and wizards only real in children's stories? Ethan used his magic hat to visit his favorite wizard to find out! Can you find at least 10 items that often show up in stories about wizards?

EXTRA FUN: Who is your favorite storybook wizard?

Moon Walk

In 1969, Ethan visited the moon with Apollo 11! Who knows where future space travelers will go? There is talk of a mission to the "red planet." Can you find the 4 letters that spell this planet's real name?

CHAPTER 6

Celebrations

Festive 4th of July

The 4th of July is when we honor the birthday of the United States. Many small towns have a celebration where everyone joins in! Can you find the 13 stars hiding in this town's parade?

Valentine's Day

Ryan is making a special card for his mom. Help him find **3 more hearts**, a **bottle of glue**, **tape**, and a **pencil**. Finally, find the six letters he will need to spell a familiar sentiment. Write the letters on the dotted lines!

_ _ _

_ _ _ _

Clowning Around

National Clown Week is celebrated in early August. What a good time to go to a circus! See if you can find the 5 props the clowns on the facing page are hiding: a **toothbrush**, **banana**, **whistle**, **rubber snake**, and **lollipop**.

EXTRA FUN: See how many letter Es (capital or small) you can also find hiding in this picture. Color them brown. When you are finished, what do you have? Check the answer key for the silly answer.

Earth Day

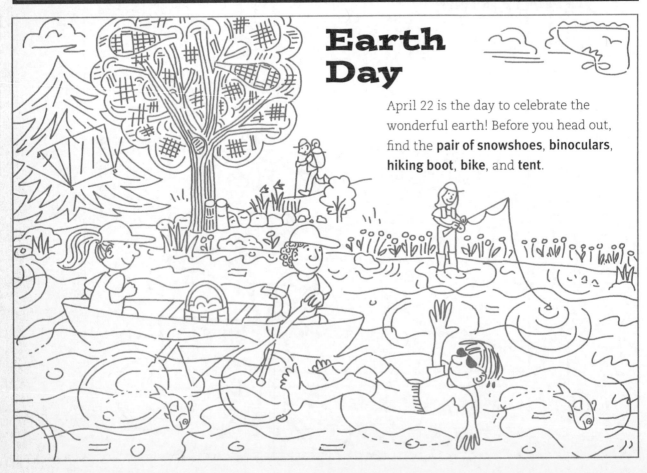

April 22 is the day to celebrate the wonderful earth! Before you head out, find the **pair of snowshoes**, **binoculars**, **hiking boot**, **bike**, and **tent**.

April Fool!

April 1st is a day for practical jokes and silly hoax! See if you can find the 12 things that are not as they should be, and the 1 thing that seems like it could be true but really isn't!

1, 2, 3 . . .

Every February the Audubon Society sponsors the Great Backyard Bird count. How many birds can you count in this backyard tree?

Egg Hunt ✿

Lots of communities celebrate Easter by sponsoring an egg hunt. Can you find 22 eggs hiding on the facing page?

★ ★ ★ ★ ★ ★ ★ ★ ★ ★ ★ ★ ★ 68 ★ ★ ★ ★ ★ ★ ★ ★ ★ ★ ★ ★ ★

Trick or Treat

Celebrating Halloween means lots of candy! Look closely to find the **5 lollipops**, **6 candy corn**, and **1 candy bar** hiding in this spooky crowd!

Chips n' Dip

March 14th is National Potato Chip Day! Celebrate by finding the 12 times the word **DIP** is hidden in this puzzle.

Twice the Fun

Krystal and Kayla think it's great that there is a Twins Festival celebrated each August in Twinsburg, Ohio!

Most days the girls wear the exact same dress and hairstyle, but today there are 6 differences. Can you find them?

CHAPTER 7

Animal Kingdom

Pack Rat

Pack rats like to collect all sorts of things and pile them into big, messy nests. These critters particularly like objects that are shiny and bright! See if you can find what this rat has been taking from his neighbors. Look for a **thimble**, **whistle**, **button**, **ring**, **comb**, **pencil**, **key**, **eyeglasses**, **paper clip**, **coin**, **fishhook**, and **fork**.

Fun fact: If a pack rat lives in the desert, he might protect his nest with cactus spines!

Monarch Butterfly

In the fall, North American monarch butterflies fly to Mexico and California to spend the winter. By the time they return home the next spring, some butterflies will have traveled up to 3,000 miles! Find 7 letters that, when you put them in the correct order, will spell a word to describe this journey.

Extra Fun: Color the large white areas in the center of the wings bright orange. Color the dark edges of the wings and body black. Leave the small spots white.

Hamster on the Loose

Oops—there are supposed to be 3 hamsters on the activity table, not just 2! Where is the other class pet hiding? See if you can find him!

Peacock

Can you find 17 things in this pretty peacock that start with the letter P?

Walrus

On summer days off the coast of Alaska, you can sometimes see thousands of male walruses basking in the sun. Thousands of walruses mean twice that number of long white tusks. What could these guys really use? A good toothbrush! See if you can find 1.

Best Friends

These two pals share everything, even their snacks! See if you can find 2 each of **chicken legs**, **fish**, **strips of bacon**, **slices of pizza**, and **dog bones**.

Great Goldfish

A fancy goldfish makes a wonderful pet that can live for many years. Check this fish tank carefully to make sure there is nothing in there that can harm Ruby the goldfish!

Panda?

While they may look cuddly, giant pandas would rather be left alone to sleep, eat bamboo, and play. See if you can find the very, very shy panda hiding on the facing page.

Aye-Aye

This little animal is called an Aye-Aye. It lives high up in the rainforests of Madagascar and only eats fruit and insects. Can you find the 6 eyes and the 5 I's in this picture of an Aye-Aye?

Rescue Dogs

Search and Rescue dogs are trained to find people who are lost in all kids of places. This dog is practicing in a forest. Can you find the 9 hidden people before Jasper the dog does?

RESCUE

Sharks, Etc.

How many sharks can you find swimming in this ocean? Count shark noses or shark tails as 1 whole shark!

Extra Fun: How many jellyfish are hiding in with the sharks? What 1 item totally doesn't belong in this picture?

CHAPTER 8

Wide, Wide World

Mexico

Piñatas (peen-YAH-tahs) are colorful paper containers filled with candy and toys. They are enjoyed by Mexican children at birthday parties and festivals.

Piñatas are hung from a tree. Children wear blindfolds and swing at the piñata with a stick. When someone breaks it open, everyone scrambles to collect the treats!

Can you find the 11 pieces of candy corn and the 7 lollipops?

France

The Eiffel Tower is one of the most famous symbols of France. It was built in 1889 for an international fair held in Paris.

Can you find the numbers 1-8-8-9 and the letters P-A-R-I-S hiding in this antique poster?

Australia

Coral reefs are found in warm, shallow, clean water. They are home to a huge variety of fish, marine animals, and sea plants. Australia's Great Barrier Reef is the largest reef of all, stretching 1,250 miles! Help this diver keep this section of reef clean and healthy by finding the **shoe**, **tin can**, **coat hanger**, **plastic bottle**, **pencil**, **glove**, **quarter**, **umbrella**, and **plastic spoon and fork**.

Russia

A matryoshka (MAT-RO-shka) is a set of hollow wooden dolls that nest one inside the other. These dolls are very popular in Russia and are painted to look like moms with children, characters from folk tales, animals, and even politicians! The matryoshka was inspired by a Japanese doll representing the seven gods of fortune. Can you find the numbers 1 through 7 hiding in this set of nesting dolls?

EXTRA FUN: Use bright-colored pencils to decorate this matryoshka.

Sweden

Swedish author Astrid Lindgren wrote a popular children's book about an unusual nine-year-old girl. Pippi Longstocking lives alone in a big house with her horse and pet monkey. Pippi is so strong that she can lift her horse over her head! See if you can find these items hiding with Pippi, Horse, and Mr. Nilsson: a **comb**, **teapot**, **wishbone**, **bubble pipe with two bubbles**, **pencil**, **jump rope**, **flag**, **banana**, **kite**, and **heart**.

Greece

Every two years, athletes from around the world travel to a different country for the Olympic games. During each competition, the athletes honor the very first Olympics, held in Greece more than 2,500 years ago! A flame is lit in Greece, then carried to wherever the current Olympics take place. The flame is used to light a torch that burns day and night while the athletes compete.

Look carefully at this torch-lighting ceremony. See if you can find the 7 stylized drawings (stick figures) that represent the sports of **volleyball**, **downhill skiing**, **cross country skiing**, **bicycle racing**, **swimming**, **soccer**, and **gymnastics**.

China

Chinese dragons may look fierce, but they are not fire-breathing monsters. These dragons are signs of wisdom, strength, and good luck! The highlight of many Chinese New Year festivals is a dragon dance. A team of dancers uses poles to hold a flowing dragon made of fabric over their heads. Find some G-O-O-D L-U-C-K hidden in this dragon dance!

India

The weather in India is hot and humid. Women stay comfortable by wearing a thin fabric garment called a sari. Saris that are worn every day are made from plain fabric, but ones worn for special events are covered with beautiful patterns, embroidery, and even tiny mirrors!

These ladies are dressed up to go to the elephant festival. Can you find the **2 elephants** hiding in the pattern of their beautiful saris?

Canada

In the forests of the Northwest, cedar trees grow straight and tall. The native tribes of Canada would cut down these trees and carve them into totem poles. Some totem poles were carved as part of a potlatch, a ceremonial feast where the host gives many gifts. Search this totem pole for a **needle and thread**, **mug**, **comb**, **ring**, **jump rope**, **arrow**, **hatchet**, **fish hook**, **cooking pot**, and **knife**.

Saudi Arabia

This Middle Eastern country is mostly sandy, hot, and dry. But nestled between two large deserts is an amazing place where there is a lot of water. The Al-Hasa oasis has always been a good place for farmers to grow date palms. Many birds make the oasis their home, too! Look for 6 birds hiding in the trees and bushes of the oasis on the facing page.

South Africa

Soccer is incredibly popular in South Africa. However, many towns don't have soccer fields or equipment. The kids play in streets and neighborhoods with whatever ball they can find, even if the stuffing is coming out of it!

See if you can find 6 brand new soccer cleats for these boys to use!

CHAPTER 9

Simply Seasons

Sweet Season

When days are warm and nights are still cold, it's time to gather sap to make maple syrup. While these sugar makers are working, see if you can find a **sheet of notebook paper**, **kite**, **house**, **crown**, **umbrella**, **needle and thread**, **Christmas stocking**, **man's face**, **rabbit**, **mug**, and **fork**.

Hoodie Hoo!

February 20 is Northern Hemisphere Hoodie-Hoo Day. At high noon (local time), citizens are asked to go outdoors and yell, "Hoodie Hoo" three times to chase away winter! While these three characters are yelling, see if you can find the 11 signs of spring: a **butterfly**, **dragonfly**, **snake**, **turtle**, **caterpillar**, **frog**, **2 tulips**, **2 daisies**, and a **bike**.

Spring Cleaning

A long, snowy winter can really make a mess of the plants in the yard and the outside of the house. Plus everyone has been tracking sand, grit, and slush in from the driveway! When spring finally arrives, it's time to give everything a good cleaning and start the season fresh and tidy.

Look for a bottle of spray cleaner, paintbrush, rake, broom, dustpan, sponge, roll of paper towels, and pair of rubber gloves.

WELCOME

FREE

Cooling Off

When the summer weather gets hot and sticky, the coolest place to be is in the pool! While these girls are enjoying their swim, see if you can find 8 other signs of summer. Look for a **sea horse**, **sailboat**, **kite**, **jump rope**, **ice cream cone**, **balloon**, **roller skate**, and **seashell**.

At the Dog Park

A beautiful summer's day is the perfect time to take your pal out for some fun! See if you can find the 6 dog biscuits these dogs are looking for.

Extra Fun: Can you find the 1 cat?

Two Scoops

There's nothing nicer on a summer day than stopping for ice cream! While these kids slurp their cones, see if you can find the **tic-tac-toe board**, **acorn**, **musical note**, **telephone receiver**, **fan**, **bunny**, **fork**, **wristwatch**, **book**, **flag**, and **letter L**.

Carving Pumpkins

Halloween is a favorite autumn holiday. These four kids (and a very bony friend) are getting ready by carving pumpkins! While they are showing off their handiwork, see if you can find these 9 items: **candle**, **teapot**, **comb**, **paperclip**, **spider**, **piece of pizza**, **light bulb**, **planet**, and **banana**.

Picking Apples

Autumn is the perfect time for picking crisp apples. There are 10 other things hiding on this tree, too! Look for a **banana**, **diamond ring**, **needle and thread**, **boot**, **candle**, **acorn**, **eye**, **fish**, **closed umbrella**, and **sailboat**.

Where Is Winter?

Most people hear the word winter and think of ice and snow. But some people live where it is warm all year round, even in the winter season! See if you can find the 10 warm and cold winter items hiding in the scenes on the facing page. Look for: **beach ball**, **cold drink with straw**, **flip flop**, **glove**, **gingerbread man**, **ice cream cone**, **ice skate**, **mitten**, **mug of hot cocoa**, and **beach umbrella**.

Yum!

Building gingerbread houses is a delicious way to have some winter fun. They are not only beautiful, but tasty, too! See if you can find the 11 times **YUM** has been used in this candy cottage.

On Ice

Start at the girl and use your finger to trace backward over the path she made across the ice. What pictures did she make? What did she write?

Look Again

You may almost be on the last page, but there are still a few more things to look for! Try to spot each of these picture pieces somewhere in this book. Write the name of the puzzle each piece is from in the space under each box. Hint: There is only one piece from each chapter!

1.

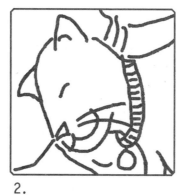

2.

3.

4.

5.

6.

7.

8.

9.

RESOURCE LIST

If you have finished this book and want to do more hidden picture puzzles, here are a few websites you will find very interesting! Some of them are animated, so the pictures dance or move while you try to find them.

www.kids-puzzles.com

These hidden picture puzzles look like ordinary black and white drawings. But when you click on a hidden object, it pops into full color and moves across the page to take its place in the list of objects you are looking for! This site also has a section of hidden picture problems, connect-the-dot puzzles, matching games, word search puzzles, and mazes. Note: Your computer will need the FLASH 6 plug-in for you to view this site. Ask an adult to help with the easy download.

www.highlightskids.com

The *Highlights for Children* website has many free hidden picture puzzles available, with no registration required. Once you get to the home page, click on the Hidden Pictures tab located in the menu down the left side of the page. Then choose the bright-orange PLAY tab. Each hidden picture puzzle has three levels of difficulty, so they are challenging for all ages!

www.niehs.nih.gov/kids/home.htm

This fun site was prepared by the National Institute of Environmental Health Sciences. From the home page, click on the link for Games and Activities. After you have found all the objects in each picture, you can color the picture online, too! Explore additional links for Sing-a-Long songs, Brainteasers and Riddles, Storytime, and Humor and Jokes. Note: Your computer will need a Java-enabled browser like Netscape or Microsoft Explorer for you to play many of these games.

www.wimzie.com

Once you get to the home page, follow the links from Kids to Wimzie Activities to Horace's Hidden Pictures. Based on characters from the popular kids TV puppet show "Wimzie's House," these puzzles are designed for younger kids.

Printed Resources

Clay Quests: Hidden Picture Puzzles by Helena Bogosian

Clay Quests features puzzles made entirely out of polymer clay. Each illustration is handcrafted to provide a colorful, three-dimensional effect that jumps off the page. Whether kids are trying to find matching socks in a messy laundry room, counting needles in a haystack, or seeking a special set of dinosaur bones on an archeological dig, they'll have to look closely to figure out these picture puzzles. Sterling Publishing Co., New York, NY, Copyright 2008.

The Ultimate Hidden Picture Puzzle Book by Joe Boddy

Published in 1990, this great puzzle book is still easily available from online booksellers. The illustrations are humorous and a bit more complex than most hidden pictures, so they are good for older kids. Ingeniously concealed objects challenge sharp-eyed sleuths to ferret out survival equipment in a jungle scene; a near-sighted giant's mislaid glasses; tools belonging to an absent-minded tree house builder; and many other items. Dover Publications, Mineola, NY, Copyright 1990.

Hidden Picture Puzzles by artist Liz Ball

Visit her website at *http://hiddenpicturepuzzles.com* to order one of her puzzle books. Topics include Frog Fun, What Job Do You See?, Merry Christmas, Bible Stories, and more. There are several pages of puzzles that you can print out and play for free!

Animal Hidden Pictures by Cheryl Nathan

This book has fourteen different hidden picture puzzles. Each puzzle features a different kind of animal, such as giraffes, lions, ostriches, rhinos, crocodiles, and more! Dover Publications, Mineola, NY, Copyright 2002.

Super Colossal Book of Hidden Pictures, Volume 2

Compiled by the editors of *Highlights* magazine, this book has over 150 pages of puzzles, with more than 2,000 objects to find! Boyds Mills Press, PA, Copyright 2001.

The Mighty Big Book of Optical Illusions by Craig Yoe

You might not think of optical illusions in the same category as hidden picture puzzles, but many of them are! Do you see a magician or a rabbit? An old lady or a pretty young girl? Is this man playing a banjo or a flute? It's all in the way you look at it! Price Stern Sloan, New York, NY, Copyright 2002.

PUZZLE SOLUTIONS

page v ★ **Introduction**

page 2 ★ **Go Fish**

page 3 ★ **Sneak Attack!**

page 4 ★ **Jump Rope**

PUZZLE SOLUTIONS

page 5 ⋆ **Ooey Gooey**

page 6 ⋆ **Round and Round**

page 7 ⋆ **Driveway Art**

page 8 ⋆ **Goal!**

PUZZLE SOLUTIONS

page 9 ★ **Choo Choo**

page 10 ★ **The Champ**

page 11 ★ **ZAP!**

There are 11 ZAPs on this page. Multiply that by 10 for a score of 110. Congratulations, you win!

page 12 ★ **Flashlight Tag**

PUZZLE SOLUTIONS

page 14 ★ **Swim Team**

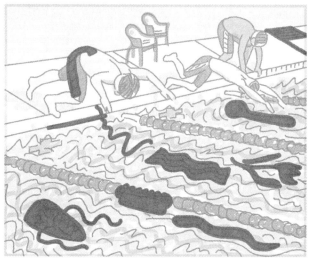

page 15 ★ **Zip Zip**

page 16 ★ **Love to Bake**

page 17 ★ **Pet Me, Please**

PUZZLE SOLUTIONS

page 18 ★ **Feed the Birds**

page 19 ★ **Fuzzy Friends**

page 20 ★ **Tumble Bug**

page 21 ★ **Making Music**

PUZZLE SOLUTIONS

page 22 ★ **Busy With Blocks**

page 23 ★ **Crazy for Quilting**

page 24 ★ **Model Kid**

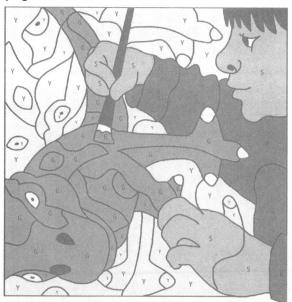

Jacob is painting a model of a dinosaur.

page 26 ★ **I Like to Help Animals**

PUZZLE SOLUTIONS

page 27 ★ **I Like to Race**

page 28 ★ **I Like to Act**

page 29 ★ **I Like to Fish**

page 30 ★ **I Like to Draw**

PUZZLE SOLUTIONS

page 31 ★ **I Like to Teach**

page 32 ★ **I Like to Fly**

page 33 ★ **I Like to Play With Hair**

page 34 ★ **I Like to See How Things Work**

PUZZLE SOLUTIONS

page 35 ★ **I Like to Save the World**

page 36 ★ **I Like to Sell Things**

page 38 ★ **Wicked Witches**

page 39 ★ **Santa´s Elves**

PUZZLE SOLUTIONS

page 40 ★ **Jack and the Giant**

page 41 ★ **Groaning Ghosts**

page 42 ★ **Under the Sea**

page 43 ★ **Uniquely Unicorn**

PUZZLE SOLUTIONS

page 44 ★ **Fairy Godmother**

page 45 ★ **Lucky Leprechauns**

page 46 ★ **Dragon's Den**

There are over 40 items hidden in this dragon's den. We have highlighted just a few for you. Keep looking!

page 47 ★ **3 Wishes**

3 FISH
3 SNAKES   6 NUMBER 3
3 BANANAS   6 COAT HANGERS

PUZZLE SOLUTIONS

page 48 ★ **Terrible Troll**

page 50 ★ **Let's Go!**

page 51 ★ **Dinosaur Days**

page 52 ★ **Ancient Egypt**

PUZZLE SOLUTIONS

page 53 ★ **Just Jousting**

page 54 ★ **Antique Car**

page 55 ★ **Great Galileo**

page 56 ★ **Mr. President**

PUZZLE SOLUTIONS

page 57 ★ **Oh, Blots!**

page 59 ★ **Magic Time**

page 58 ★ **Is Anybody Home?**

page 60 ★ **Moon Walk**

PUZZLE SOLUTIONS

page 62 ★ **Festive 4th of July**

page 63 ★ **Valentine's Day**

page 64 ★ **Earth Day**

PUZZLE SOLUTIONS

page 65 ★ Clowning Around

When you color the six E's brown, you end up with half a dozen "brownies"!

page 66 ★ April Fool!

The story about Swiss spaghetti farmers was aired on the British news on April 1, 1957. Hundreds of people called the tv station to find out how they cold grow their own spaghetti trees!

page 67 ★ And Many More . . .

Gramps is 89!

page 68 ★ 1, 2, 3, . . .

PUZZLE SOLUTIONS

page 69 ★ **Egg Hunt**

page 70 ★ **Trick or Treat**

page 71 ★ **Chips n' Dip**

page 72 ★ **Twice the Fun**

PUZZLE SOLUTIONS

page 74 ★ **Pack Rat**

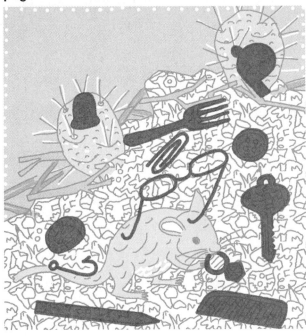

page 75 ★ **Monarch Butterfly**

AMAZING

page 76 ★ **Hamster on the Loose**

page 77 ★ **Peacock**

PAIR OF PANTS, PANSY, PAPERCLIP, PARACHUTE, PATCH, PAW PRINT, PEANUT, PEAR, PENGUIN, PENNY, PIECE OF PIE, PIG, PIN, POSTAGE STAMP, POT, PURSE, PUSHPIN

PUZZLE SOLUTIONS

page 78 ★ **Walrus**

page 79 ★ **Best Friends**

page 80 ★ **Great Goldfish**

page 81 ★ **Panda?**

It is easier to find the shy panda if you turn the puzzle page upside-down!

PUZZLE SOLUTIONS

page 82 ★ **Aye-Aye**

page 83 ★ **Rescue Dogs**

page 84 ★ **Sharks, Etc.**

There are 24 sharks and 7 jellyfish. The sock is the item that doesn't belong!

page 86 ★ **Mexico**

PUZZLE SOLUTIONS

page 87 ★ **France**

page 88 ★ **Australia**

page 89 ★ **Russia**

page 90 ★ **Sweden**

PUZZLE SOLUTIONS

page 91 ★ Greece

volleyball   downhill skiing   cross country skiing   swimming

gymnastics   bicycle racing   soccer

page 92 ★ China

page 93 ★ India

page 94 ★ Canada

PUZZLE SOLUTIONS

page 95 ★ **Saudi Arabia**

page 96 ★ **South Africa**

page 98 ★ **Sweet Season**

page 99 ★ **Hoodie Hoo!**

PUZZLE SOLUTIONS

page 100 ★ **Spring Cleaning**

page 101 ★ **Cooling Off**

page 102 ★ **At the Dog Park**

page 103 ★ **Two Scoops**

PUZZLE SOLUTIONS

page 104 ★ **Carving Pumpkins**

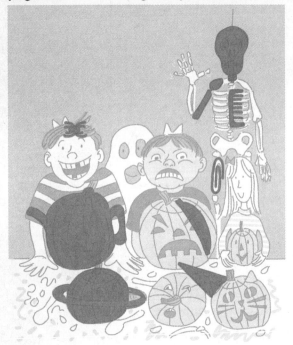

page 105 ★ **Picking Apples**

page 106 ★ **Yum!**

page 107 ★ **Where Is Winter?**

PUZZLE SOLUTIONS

page 108 ★ **On Ice**

page 109 ★ **Look Again**

1. Driveway Art

2. Pet Me, Please!

3. I Like to Save the World

4. Under the Sea

5. Dinosaur Days

6. And Many More

7. Hamster on the Loose

8. Russia

9. Sweet Season

We Have

EVERYTHING
on Anything!

With more than 19 million copies sold, the Everything® series has become one of America's favorite resources for solving problems, learning new skills, and organizing lives. Our brand is not only recognizable—it's also welcomed.

The series is a hand-in-hand partner for people who are ready to tackle new subjects—like you!

For more information on the Everything® series, please visit *www.adamsmedia.com*

The Everything® list spans a wide range of subjects, with more than 500 titles covering 25 different categories:

Business	History	Reference
Careers	Home Improvement	Religion
Children's Storybooks	Everything Kids	Self-Help
Computers	Languages	Sports & Fitness
Cooking	Music	Travel
Crafts and Hobbies	New Age	Wedding
Education/Schools	Parenting	Writing
Games and Puzzles	Personal Finance	
Health	Pets	